D0984596

SAM SNEAD ON GOLF

SAM SNEAD ON GOLF

by **SAM SNEAD**

photographs by **Charles Yerkow**

PRENTICE-HALL, INC.

Englewood Cliffs, N.J.

CONTENTS

SAM SNEAD ON GOLF

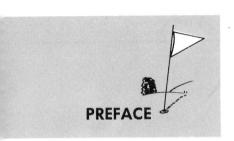
THE MAN CALLED SLAMMIN' SAM

by Oscar Fraley

Samuel Jackson Snead, the man they call "Slammin' Sam," is a living legend in the world of golf.

He has been called "the greatest natural golfer in the history of the game."

Perennial idol of the galleries as well as the players' player, Sam has won more tournaments than any player

1

in the annals of competitive golf. As this is being written, he has captured more than 100 championships.

The man with the "sweetest swing in golf" has been a sensation ever since he came striding out of the Virginia hills in 1936 to hurtle to the top of the heap.

He has won three P.G.A. championships. Three times he has captured the coveted Masters. His long list of triumphs include the British Open Championship and just about everything else you can name—except the U.S. Open.

Four times he has been second in that one, and yet even those tragic failures have helped Sam captivate the galleries in a manner no other golfer ever could. They proved he was human and swept him into the hearts of the world's hackers and low handicap players alike.

Another time he blew the Open with a horrendous eight which still reverberates throughout the world of golf, and probably always will. That was at Philadelphia's Spring Mill Course in 1939, the day of my first association with him.

I have heard literally thousands of people describe how they saw Sam chop out that "big eight." Actually, there was only a comparative handful of spectators around the young hill-billy when he teed off on the 72nd and final hole at Spring Mill that afternoon needing a par five to win the Open and a bogey six to tie.

You will get a kick out of his own description of that eight, just as I did, as he recounts it in his chapter on the psychological side of golf and how to "blue-print" your game. Had Sam blue-printed his final hole that day, I am certain that, as he claims, he well might have won four or five Open championships.

But my most vivid memory of that day is the pressurized moment when a seething Sam, sitting disgustedly in front of his locker, was asked by a brash reporter:

"Sam, just what happened to make you take that eight?"

The sportswriter well could have worn a sand wedge, buried in his cranium, for the remainder of his days.

But Sam's inherent humor saved the day. He gasped back the bitterness and then, with a rueful smile, replied in a slow drawl:

"I don't know. But I sure would like to play that hole over again."

Sam has been almost a hobby with me ever since that moment.

He has that indefinable something called "color." Just as baseball players stop in their warmup tasks to watch Ted Williams take his licks at the batting cage, so do Sam's fellow professionals halt their own practice to watch him hit his tuneup shots. And Sam's own tolerance of the galleries is a rarity in these days of jittery-nerved competitors who glare angrily at the first sign of a cough or sneeze from the sidelines.

They tell more stories about the colorful Sam than they do about any other golfer. One of the earliest concerned his first major victory, in the 1937 Oakland Open. The next day, Fred Corcoran, at that time the P.G.A. tournament director, took Sam an air mail copy of the *New York Times* which contained an account of Snead's first win and also carried Sam's picture.

"Now how did they ever get my picture?" wondered the wide-eyed Sam, "Why, I ain't never been to New York in my whole life."

There still is much of that naivete in Samuel Jackson Snead, which probably is much of his appeal. And he never has lost that taste for triumph.

His record, in addition to his tournament victories, is amazing. Four times he has won the Vardon Trophy, which goes annually to the golfer with the low scoring average over the entire year. Capturing it in 1950, he set a record scoring average of 69.23 strokes per round. He has been on eight Ryder Cup teams and in 1949 was named the Professional Golfer of the Year.

Despite his casual nonchalance on the course, Sam still manages the extreme concentration which turns other golfers into grim-faced automatons. But the smile is usually there, even if he doesn't hear what you're saying.

Such as the time during a tournament round when Corcoran approached and told Sam that Bing Crosby, one of Snead's long-time golfing pals, had won the Academy Award.

"That's nice," Sam replied absent-mindedly, "was it match or medal?"

And nothing to me better typifies his competitive spirit than the occasion when he broke his wrist in 1946 sliding into second base during a soft ball game with a group of caddies at his Greenbrier Club in White Sulphur Springs, West Virginia.

A friend, referring to the shock of sustaining the fracture, asked solicitously whether Sam had lost consciousness.

"Were you out?" he asked.

"Out?" Sam snorted. "Hell, no, I wasn't out. I was safe!"

Sam is a natural athlete. He is an ardent fisherman and

hunter. As a schoolboy he was a track, basketball and football star who attracted a number of college scholarship offers. As a pitcher he struck out 18 men in one game and he was also something of a boxer.

But Sam decided after high school that he would make golf his career and the loss to those other sports has been golf's gain. For, as the immortal Bobby Jones said:

"Sam has the best swing I've ever seen."

Millions of others saw it, and agreed, as the Slammer made a one-man parade of television's 1958 All-Star golf show, winning thirteen matches in a row and setting a record $28,000 in winnings as he turned back the world's best.

In this book, Slammin' Sam blueprints that "sweetest swing" as well as all the other know-how he has gathered over the years so that you, too, can be a winner.

SAM SNEAD'S
TOURNAMENT VICTORIES

Golfer of the year (1949)

All-time leading money winner.

Vardon Trophy Winner (1938-1949-1950-1955)

Ryder Cup Team (1937-1947-1949-1951-1953-1955)

British Open (1946)

Masters (1949-1952-1954)

P.G.A. (1942-1949-1951)

All-American Open (1952)

World Championship (1946)

Argentine Open (1942)

Insurance City Open (1955)

Inverness Four Ball (1938-1940)

Inverness Round Robin (1950-1952)

Jacksonville Open (1945-1946)

Julius Boros Open (1952)

La Gorce Individual (1954)

Los Angeles Open (1945-1950)

Miami Open (1937-1939-1946-1950-1951-1955)

Miami Beach Open (1950)

Miami Biltmore Four Ball (1939)

Nassau Open (1937)

Canadian Open (1938-1940-1941)

Panama Open (1954)

Western Open (1949-1950)

Anthracite Open (1940)

Baton Rouge Open (1953)

Bayshore Individual (1955)

Bing Crosby Tournament (1937-1938-1941)

Bing Crosby Pro-Am (1947)

Boca Raton Open (1956)

Chicago Open (1938)

Colonial Invitation (1950)

Dallas Open (1945-1957-1958)

Dapper Dan Open (1949)

Decatur Open (1949)

Eastern Open (1952)

Goodall Round Robin (1938-1952)

Greenbrier Open (1951-1952-1953-1958)

Greenbrier Pro-Am (1951)

Greensboro Open (1938-1946-1949-1950-1955-1956)

Gulfport Open (1945)

Havana Invitation (1948)

Havana Pro-Am (1948)

Henry Hurst Invitation (1941)

National Celebrities (1949)

North-South Open (1941-1950)

Oakland Open (1937)

Ontario Open (1939)

Orlando Two Ball (1953)

Palm Beach Round Robin (1954-1955-1957)

Pensacola Open (1945)

Portland Open (1944)

Reading Open (1950)

Richmond Open (1944)

Rochester Open (1941)

St. Augustine Pro-Am (1941)

St. Paul Open (1937)

St. Petersburg Open (1939-1941-1942)

Seminole Individual (1952)

Seminole Pro-Am (1948)

Texas Open (1948-1950)

Tulsa Open (1945)

Virginia Open (1946)

Washington Star Open (1949)

West Virginia Closed Pro (1936)

West Virginia Open (1948)

West Virginia P.G.A. (1948)

Westchester Open (1938)

White Sulphur Springs Open (1938)

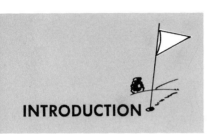

LEARN IT, THEN FORGET IT

Playing golf is like eating. It's something which has to come naturally.

When you were a child, you had to learn how to hold a spoon; then a fork and a knife. Finally you mastered them and now you handle them automatically.

Now if you think about bending your elbow when you eat you just might poke yourself in the eye.

It's the same way with golf.

Naturally you have to learn the various parts of a golf swing. But once you get it, don't think about your swing anymore. If you do, you maybe won't poke yourself in the eye, but you'll sure ruin your swing.

All I'm leading up to is that you CAN play good golf if you master the fundamentals, get them all working together—and then forget about them.

That's the trouble with most players when they get up on the tee. They try to remember too many separate bits of instruction instead of already having them geared together and just firing away.

Eye on the ball, they'll tell themselves . . . Slow backswing . . . Straight left arm . . . Easy pivot . . . Pause at the top of the backswing . . . Hit from the inside out . . . Snap those wrists through the ball . . . Pronate the hands on the follow through . . . Keep the head down until the swing is finished . . . and so on through a miserable, soul-searing afternoon.

What they are doing is poking themselves in the eye because they are thinking about how they should eat.

What I'm aiming at in this book is to eliminate this herky-jerky approach to the game of golf. Too many people tackle this game as if they were going out to spend an afternoon in a torture chamber.

They do this because they haven't taken the time to practice long enough to get their swing all into one piece.

Naturally, all of those things they keep telling themselves are necessary.

You do need the slow backswing, the straight left arm, the easy pivot, the tiny pause at the top of the backswing, the inside out swing, the snap of the wrists. Of course you have to keep your head down and your eye on the ball— simply because when you look up you pull your swing out of its groove.

But when you step onto the first tee, all of this should have been driven back into your subconscious. Develop the mechanics, rhythm and timing into one smooth, easy swing.

Right here would be the perfect spot to go into the business of being relaxed.

Golf is a game you play for fun. So have fun playing it by loosening up, not tightening up, when you step out on the course.

How, you may ask, do I relax? The answer is somewhat difficult to put across. It's the difference between a soldier standing at attention and being "at ease." You don't want your body stiff, every muscle rigid, and yet you don't want to be so close to collapse that a shove would push you off your feet. You want the poised whippiness of a man using a fly rod.

Take a deep breath just before you step up to your shot and momentarily extend your club out in front of you at eye level after you have taken your grip to loosen your shoulder muscles, as you see many pro golfers—and many baseball players—do when they are getting ready to hit.

The full answer is to be comfortable. If you aren't, then you are too tight and tense.

Being tense ruins more golf shots for more players than anything else I know. If and when you are all tightened up you just aren't giving yourself a chance to swing properly at the ball.

Tenseness causes a lot of difficulties but the worst is that it forces you into hurrying and harrying your backswing. When you do this, you're tossing everything out of gear. That fast backswing throws you off balance and out of the groove so badly that it inspired the hustler's ancient slogan:

"Give me a man with a fast backswing and a fat wallet."

Even fine players unconsciously drop into this rhythm-ruining rush of the backswing on occasion. Bobby Jones was having a terrible time just before the start of the 1925 National Open. He was playing so badly that he sent for Stewart Maiden, the old Scots pro at his home course. Maiden silently watched Jones hit two bags of practice balls and then observed caustically:

"Why don't you try hittin' the ball wi' your backswing?"

A little thing, yet Jones, rushing his backswing unconsciously, had thrown off his whole game. He didn't win the Open. But with his backswing slowed he did play well enough to tie Willie Macfarlane before losing the playoff.

This bears out the fact that rhythm and timing are, above all, the most important facets of the swing. You can't have them, or even come close to having them, if you aren't relaxed. It is a relaxation which must take over the whole body. By this, as I said, I don't mean that you should be on the verge of collapse. It is simply that your whole body, especially through the legs, must be loose and easy.

Walter Hagen always said that as long as he kept his legs relaxed he didn't worry. It was his theory—and I agree one hundred per cent—that with his legs relaxed, the rest of his body would take care of itself.

It makes sense. Because when your legs and ankles are supple, then your muscles all can do the work you want them to do. Only then can you pivot correctly and get that sense of rhythm and timing which helps you to go back in one piece and start down from the top with everything working in close harmony.

In this connection, I feel that I have been mighty lucky. I have always been blessed with a loose, easy swing ever since I started swishing a hickory stick at acorns when I was a kid. Sometimes things go haywire even for us professionals. When that happens we have to do the same thing you should do—get out on the practice tee and analyze the swing piece by piece. It doesn't take long to figure out what is going wrong. Once you work that one unmeshed cog into its proper place in the machinery of the golf swing you're back in business.

But once you do get your swing grooved again, forget the piece-meal mechanics. This is the place to strive for the winning rhythm and let the re-grooved swing take care of itself.

In this book we will consider these cogs in their proper order to teach you the winning golf swing from start to finish. You'll find out that it isn't a complicated series of do's and don'ts but actually is one sweeping motion.

As a helpful innovation, you will find inverted drawings of the grip and stances. This, I believe, will give you a previously ignored perspective which you should have when you are looking down at your shots.

A great deal has been written about how to play golf. Let me make it clear right from the start that the ideal way to learn to play is by taking in-person lessons from a qualified professional.

Everyone doesn't have the time, or in other cases, the money, to do this. Those people are the ones I want to help. And you can learn a great deal from between the covers of this book, particularly by studying the illustrations.

After all, Walter J. Travis began to learn golf out of instruction books at the age of 35. Four years later, in 1900, he won the U.S. Amateur Golf Championship. He won it again in 1901 and 1903 and, in 1904, became the first foreigner to win the British Amateur Championship.

I won't promise any such results. But with proper application and a certain amount of practice you can play good golf.

In golf there are three vitally important phases. You have to start off with the proper grip. Next you must take the proper stance. Then there is the swing.

Put them together on the practice tee or range. *Memorize* each facet *with your muscles.* Then just *relax* and *swing it.*

You don't think about eating. So groove your golf swing and forget it.

Why poke yourself in your golfing eye?

Sam Snead

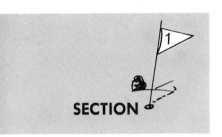

SECTION

EQUIPMENT
AND BASIC PRINCIPLES

You are allowed, under the rules of golf, to carry four-teen clubs in your bag.

For the golfer who plays it "by the book," this means four woods, the driver or number one wood; the brassie or number two wood for the longest fairway shots; the spoon or number three wood, and the number four wood.

Then there are nine irons and a putter. Making up the irons are the long irons, the number two and number three; the medium irons, meaning the numbers four, five and six irons, and the short irons, which are the seven, eight and nine irons. To these you add a wedge, which is a heavy-soled club used for playing out of sand or deep rough or for those biting, quick-stopping "sit down" pitch shots to the green.

Many professionals vary this selection by omitting certain clubs which they do not play well or for other reasons. As example, some tournament players like to carry two wedges, one for the rough and for approach shots, and the other a particularly heavy-soled "blaster" to handle bad trap lies. Others may carry two putters or feel better with a special chipping iron.

Naturally, something has to be left behind to meet the 14-club limit.

Some discard their drivers. Others leave out the brassie. Still others dispose of the two iron. The personal combinations are almost endless.

What I'm coming to is that it is my personal feeling that the casual or "weekend" golfer would do far better playing with "weekend" equipment.

CLUBS TO AVOID

My suggestion, if you don't have a great deal of time for practice and are able to play only once or twice a week, or even less, is to eliminate the number one driver, the number two wood or brassie and the two and three irons.

In their place obtain a one and one-half wood and a five wood, a four for two trade which will pay great dividends on your scorecard.

The 100 shooter makes too many mistakes with the driver, which can be an instrument of Satan if you aren't swinging just right. A lot of duffers, feeling that the brassie is easier to handle, will use the number two wood off the tee.

What they are forgetting is that, barring a precision swing, the face of the brassie is too shallow for use off a wooden tee. In this case the odds are that you will be skying the ball and losing a lot of precious distance.

The brassie also is a dangerous fairway club unless you have a practically perfect lie. The slight bit of distance it gives you over the number three or four woods is slight compensation when you consider the gamble involved.

THE ONE AND ONE-HALF WOOD

In place of the driver and the brassie, I would suggest a one and one-half wood. This club is not a brassie. It's the normal, deeper-faced driver but it has more loft added and gives more assurance of getting the ball safely off the wooden tee.

Once off the tee, you have the three and four woods for your longer fairway shots. And remember, barring a perfect lie, again give yourself all the help possible by playing the loftier four wood. A safe rule is, when in doubt, to play the four wood even over the three wood or spoon.

THE FIVE WOOD

The five wood is a relatively new innovation for general use and takes the place of the two and three irons.

It requires a great deal of practice to learn to play the two and three irons adeptly. Because of their long shafts and lack of loft, these long irons require an extraordinary timing, one far too exacting for the average golfer.

The five wood does their job and with far less margin for error. The flat sole of the five wood slides through the turf, instead of digging into it as the long irons must. You'll find that its weight and sliding factor make it a fine club for the average golfer to play.

THE WEDGE

This can be the best club in your bag, with only a minimum of practice, and the greatest stroke saver of them all. It will dig a ball out of impenetrable rough; blast the ball out of traps when it is buried in the sand and make the ball bite to a stop near the flag when you have lost a shot along the way and need to get up close for a saving one-putt.

The wedge is the greatest stroke-saving development of modern times, whether you are a demon player or a duffer, and I am constantly surprised at the number of players who still go along without using one.

This club is the principal reason why scoring generally has been lowered so fantastically since the Jones era, even though courses on the whole are longer and tougher.

There is a combination wedge. However, if you reduce the number of clubs you carry by substituting the one and one-half wood and the five wood for your driver, brassie and two and three irons, you will be inside the maximum number of clubs allowed if you have both a sand wedge and a pitching wedge in your bag. They will be well worth the investment.

The major reason for carrying a pitching wedge, as I see it, is that the average golfer has to do his best shot-making from 50 yards into the pin. Most players, even the average and weekend kind, hit the ball far enough off the tee and through the fairway to have a chance to score well. They may not hit the real long ball associated with top flight golf but, then, they aren't expected to smack it out there 250 to 300 yards.

But the pitching wedge, with a bit of practice, can make up for the shot which the duffer wastes while getting within striking distance of the green.

It's from 50 yards in to the flag that the pitching wedge will give you a better chance of getting close enough for a saving one-putt than the eight or nine iron pitches. That's because the pitching wedge makes the ball bite and hold the green where the other approach irons let the ball run too much on many occasions.

Former Vice President Richard Nixon wasn't able to break a hundred a few years back and he just couldn't understand why not. The answer was that he was wasting shots here and there getting to within that 50-yard radius of the green. Then he was pitching up and two-putting. I advised him to practice his chip shots with a wedge.

Now, pitching and chipping better than he ever did, he is in the 80's. He doesn't over-run the green as before and, where he once did hold the green but for two putts, he now sticks it up close enough to the pin for a chance to hole out in one.

Yet, as former President Eisenhower proved by his much-publicized pitching on the White House lawn to improve his short game, you must practice the shot to gain any sort of consistency.

This need for practice holds with all of us. When a professional lays off from competitive golf for any length of time, it is his short game which goes first. I know personally that after a layoff I still can hit those long shots because my swing is grooved from memory and my rhythm is undisturbed.

It's the short game, with its demand for so much "feel," which is the most difficult to recapture and which requires so much more work.

Intelligent practice is necessary, too. The professional, before starting a round, goes to the practice tee and works his way completely through his bag of clubs. Start with your short irons and work up through your medium irons, long irons and woods, hitting balls with each one in progression until you have the "feel" of the club. Then, just before teeing off, tune up your putting touch for about fifteen minutes on the putting green. You'll find it pays terrific dividends.

SWINGWEIGHTS

Before moving on from equipment, let me say that I don't consider swingweight too important and I feel that the average golfer worries too much about it.

Swingweights range from C-0, the lightest swingweight, to D-9, the heaviest. This is a scale which, simplified, represents the pull of the weight in the clubhead on your arm. Thus the medium swingweight for the average golfer is a D-2 or a D-3. My irons are D-5 or D-6 and my woods are a bit heavier.

Good golfers often don't have the slightest idea what swingweight they are using. The swingweight to use is the one where you, personally, can "feel" the clubhead when you swing the club.

LENGTH OF SHAFTS

The length of your shafts should depend on your height and the length of your arms, which means that it's a good idea to have your clubs tailor-fitted by a good professional.

Generally speaking, however, the standard lengths are acceptable for those from five feet, nine inches to six feet tall. The standard length is a 43-inch shaft for the driver and a 38⅝-inch shaft on the two iron, grading down three-eighths of an inch in each set. In other words, the three iron has a shaft three-eighths of an inch shorter than the two iron; the four iron has a shaft three-eighths of an inch shorter than the three iron, etc.

If you are tall and have abnormally short arms, then naturally you need a club with a longer shaft so that you won't have to lean over too far and spoil your balance. Shafts in woods are available up to 50 inches and in irons up to 43½ inches, grading downward as far as necessary.

There is a school of thought that the longer the shaft, the longer the arc of the swing and therefore the longer the ball will be struck. I don't hold with this. It is my feeling that you should have yourself fitted for a length suited to your stature and that the resultant perfect timing and unwasted power will give you your greatest distance.

These shafts also come in three general strengths: stiff, regular and whippy. Which you use depends on your strength, the speed of your swing and the "feel." Generally speaking a strong person with a fast swing should use the stiff shaft. The regular or semi-stiff shaft is best for the average person and for the older player who has difficulty generating speed the extra snap of the whippy shaft can be a great asset.

GRIPS

Concerning the thickness of the grip, I suggest a built up grip for those with large hands; the ordinary grip for the person with average hands, and the very small grip such as the ladies grip for those with small hands.

PLAY RIGHTHANDED

There are several schools of thought on whether a natural lefthander would switch and play golf right-handed.

I'm one of those who believes that you would do better righthanded. It is relatively easy to change over and I have seen many lefthanders convert themselves and, playing righthanded, beat their old lefthanded scores within a month's time.

Suffice it to say that Ben Hogan changed from playing lefthanded to being a righthander on the golf course. His record speaks volumes for the benefits of playing right-handed.

HIT IT STRAIGHT

It seems odd to me that one of the first things a new golfer has a desire to learn is how to hook or fade the ball.

The hook is a ball which curves from right to left and the slice is a ball traveling from left to right in flight.

Take my advice and learn to hit it straight.

Later, if you have the time for long practice sessions, you can experiment with hooking or fading the ball. It's fun, but it isn't for the beginner because you can throw your whole game out of gear.

Remember, that even the pros still are trying to be able to hit it straight every time they want to.

For the advanced golfer determined to experiment with these types of shots, however, I must hold that the hook is preferable to the fade.

I've done fairly well with a predominant hook ball and I honestly believe that Ben Hogan and Byron Nelson were playing their best when they used the hook instead of the fade to which they shifted later.

However, unless properly controlled, the hook will get you into a fair amount of trouble, which is why I advocate that you stick to hitting it straight.

THE WAGGLE

Getting along to the basic principles of golf, I'd first like to advise you to spend anywhere from fifteen minutes to a half hour on the practice tee and the putting green before you start your round. You probably have waited all week to get in this one round of golf. Too many players rush out from the office, hastily change clothes and charge straight to the first tee.

You don't ever see an airplane pilot turn over his motor and take right off, do you? Of course not. He warms up the motor first.

That's what you should do. Spend a few minutes taking the armchair kinks out of your muscles. Loosen up by swinging the club back and forth so that your swing falls into its groove. After that take the time to hit a few practice balls with your woods and your irons. Then, after a brief chipping session, just before teeing off spend a few minutes on the putting green to regain your touch.

These few minutes of concentrated attention, getting the "feel" of your clubs again after a long period of inactivity, will be reflected happily on your scorecard.

Even after you have started your round, don't get into the habit of walking up to the ball, taking a hurried stance and firing away. If you do, you are using a cold motor once again.

On the other hand, many golfers spend too much time preparing to hit their shots. They delay too long in sizing up their shot and then waste a lot more time deciding which club they should use. After this they dally even longer by taking several practice swings before moving to the ball and taking their stance. This is an entirely unnecessary delay.

You can size up your shot as you walk toward your ball and when you reach it you should already have an idea as to what club you are going to use.

At that point, as you take your stance, you can warm up your motor with a few "waggles." Instead of starting your club from a dead stop, keep your hands in motion and move the club slowly back and forth above the ball and along the line of flight. This will eliminate tension. It will also give you a feel of the clubhead. Then, after a pause to line the clubhead up behind the ball, you can slide into your swing with smooth, easy rhythm.

STAY RELAXED

One of the major faults among the weekend golfers which I have noticed particularly is that they are too tense when they address the ball and constantly hit the ball with the heel of the club.

The reason for this is that they tie themselves up into a tightly-bunched muscular knot in an effort to "knock the cover off the ball." These over-tense players stretch their arms out rigidly and, using a violent swing, rush violently down at the ball with a lunge which carries the clubhead outside of the groove.

In addressing the ball, your arms should be comfortably flexed. And you won't hit the ball with the heel of the club if you address the ball slightly off the toe of the club. During the swing, the arms naturally will extend themselves to some degree. This automatic stretching—without any conscious effort on your part—will bring the center of the clubhead directly into the ball.

Many fine players, among them Bobby Jones, Tommy Armour and Mike Turnesa, used this method of address. A few trials will tell you just how much "stretch room" you should allow for your individual swing. Maybe you don't need any, if your swing is well grooved, but if you are heeling the ball, or extending your arms too far and tying yourself up, it may be just what the doctor ordered.

STRAIGHT LEFT ARM

Here we have one of the greatest faults of the average golfer. This is the "breaking" of the left arm either at the top of the backswing or as the downswing is started.

The left arm is the controlling factor in the good golf swing.

Its role begins at address with the left arm comfortably extended—but definitely not rigid. It remains firm and extended throughout the backswing, enabling you to maintain the perfect wide arc which builds up power and grooves the swing.

Too many golfers permit the left arm to collapse as they start the downswing. At this point they allow the right hand, arm and side to take charge of making the shot. When the right side takes charge, the club moves outside the correct line or groove and is pulled back across the line of flight in contacting the ball. This is why so many weekend golfers are cursed with a slice.

So remember to keep that left arm comfortably extended and in command of the swing.

Another factor which causes a slice, and which will be gone into in greater length later, is the slight opening of the fingers of the left hand at the top of the backswing. As the downswing is started, the hand is tightened unconsciously. This causes the clubhead to loop as you start your downswing and throws it across the line of flight to cause a slice. So keep those left fingers firm at the top of the backswing—feeling the firmness with the key little finger—and save yourself a lot of headaches.

THE RIGHT ELBOW

One of the hacker's most widespread faults is raising his right elbow away from the body during the backswing. This also causes the right side to take charge of the shot and robs you of much of your hitting power.

Assuming that your grip and stance are correct, you may be going wrong here.

One gimmick to help correct this fault is to tie a knot in the middle of a small towel and hold the knot under your right armpit. To keep the towel from falling to the ground as you go into your backswing, you will be forced to keep the right elbow in fairly close to your right side— where it should be. And, if you keep the right elbow where it belongs, in against the right side, your left arm and side have to take the club back as they should.

THE LEFT HEEL

Another chief fault among those who play too infrequently is the habit of raising the left heel too far off the ground on the backswing. I have seen players lift their heel as much as five or six inches and it just has to pull their heads "off the ball" at the top of the backswing.

You will rarely see a professional golfer who lifts his left heel more than an inch and a half or two inches off the ground and from the six iron through the wedge most of them play the shot without the heel leaving the ground at all. Actually there are a great number of professional players who never permit the left heel to leave the ground on any of their shots.

Personally, in making my fullest pivot I raise the left heel about an inch and a half. This permits me to wind up fully but I am not over-reaching and thereby losing my balance and my groove as well as my consistency and firmness at impact.

PRACTICE INTELLIGENTLY

Most golfers, particularly those who take their licks on a driving range, are virtually wasting their time.

They spray their shots from one side of the range to the other and figure that, if the ball doesn't have a tail on it, they are hitting their shots well. Then they can't understand why, when they go out on the golf course, they wind up in so much trouble.

The answer is that they haven't helped themselves on the practice range.

They forget that the range is wide open while most fairways are only about 40 yards wide.

So when you practice, particularly on a driving range, pick out a target. It can be a tree or a distance marker. Then concentrate on hitting your shots within a 20-yard area on either side of the target. This will make your practice valuable and not merely a slugging session in which you are fostering bad habits which will be more difficult to correct later.

I hope that these preliminaries have given you valuable tips on the principal elements which you should look for in the chapters to come. Some of them will bear repeating. But these which we have considered are the basic principles of hitting a golf ball properly. If you commit them to memory it will make the game a pleasure to learn, instead of the task too many players discover it to be.

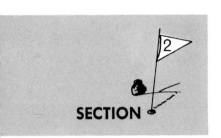

SECTION

THE GRIP

Before you ever start swinging a golf club there is one thing you must implant firmly in your mind.

That is the proper grip.

It is impossible to play good golf without a proper grip. The reason should be obvious. It is only through complete coordination of the hands that you can transmit the full power of your body to the clubhead.

Positioning the left hand, the club rests diagonally across the hand.

The left hand in place, club boxed inside the fist and the "V" of thumb and forefinger pointing over the right shoulder.

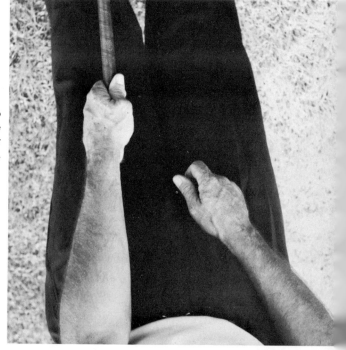

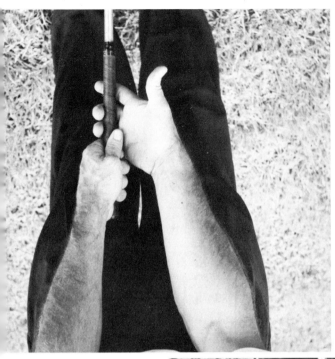

The right hand grip, with the thumb and first three fingers snugged up close to the left hand, the little finger overlapping the left forefinger.

Both hands in position, with the "V's" of both thumbs and forefingers pointing over the right shoulder.

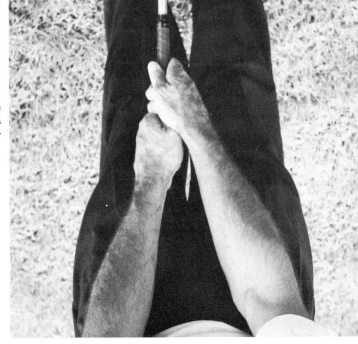

There are several ways to hold the club. Some use the "baseball grip" and there have been players who scored very well this way, notably tournament professional Bob Rosburg. The danger here is that, if you don't have perfect timing, the right hand will overpower the left hand.

The grip which I endorse, and which is used almost exclusively by championship players, is the overlapping grip which first was popularized by the great Harry Vardon. The overlapping grip to my mind makes the hands work together more than any other.

THE RIGHT WAY

Most players start off badly by grasping the club incorrectly with the fingers of the left hand.

Keep in mind that the club is not held in the fingers of the left hand but is boxed inside the fist with pressure exerted by the little finger. The club thus rests diagonally across the hand. The "V" formed by the left thumb and forefinger points directly over the RIGHT shoulder.

There is a general tendency to "open" the left hand, that is to have the "V" formed by thumb and forefinger pointing to the left shoulder. Turning the hand over a bit so that the "V" points to the RIGHT shoulder may feel somewhat uncomfortable at first but you will find that it keeps the left hand working throughout the stroke.

This is where I must admonish you again to keep that little finger of the left hand tightly closed throughout, and particularly at the top of the backswing!

If you relax that little finger at the top of your backswing you will let the clubhead drop. Then, as you start

Underside view of the favored Vardon grip, showing how the little finger of the right hand overlaps the forefinger of the left hand.

the downswing, your fist automatically will tighten up and force the clubhead to loop. It is a fault which cannot help but throw the clubhead out of its groove.

In the accompanying photos, you will note that the grip with the right hand is a complete finger grip. The grip is with the thumb and first three fingers of the right hand, snugged up close to the left hand, with the little finger of the right hand overlapping the left forefinger.

The "V" formed by the thumb and forefinger of the right hand should be parallel to the "V" formed by the left thumb and forefinger. The right thumb is about one-quarter over the top of the shaft toward the left shoulder. This also helps restrain the right hand from taking over and allows free, coordinated play with both hands.

When the left hand is placed properly, two knuckles are plainly visible on that hand. All you see of the right hand is the thumb and forefinger.

BAD GRIPS

You face all kinds of difficulties if your grip isn't properly positioned.

As an example, if you hold the club in the fingers of the left hand, instead of boxing it inside your fist, the left hand doesn't have enough power to restrain the right hand and keep it working in close harmony. The right hand then takes over and overpowers the guiding left hand and everything bad can happen: slices, pop-ups and wasted power.

Then, again, if the hands are turned too far over to the right, the clubhead will be closed (club face tilted too much forward) when the hands swing through the ball. This will smother the shot. If the hands are too far over to the left, the club face will open (tilt too far backward) and push the shot. You can test this on the practice tee, using a free, easy swing and noting the end action of the ball.

INTERLOCKING GRIP

There are a number of professionals, including Gene Sarazen, who have favored the interlocking grip. They regard it as an aid to people with small hands.

To use the interlocking grip, the hands are placed on the shaft in the same manner as in the overlapping grip.

The difference is that the left forefinger is interlaced with the little finger of the right hand.

The great majority of the playing professionals use the overlapping grip, however, and practically all of the teaching professionals favor it over the interlocking method.

If you use the overlapping grip which I have described in a correct manner, you have the basis for good golf. And, to emphasize the need for a good grip, in which you hold the club firmly but still keep the wrists pliable and flexible, remember that this one grip is the foundation for all of your shots except on the putting green.

THE WOODS

The woods, to all of us, are the thrill clubs of golf. Even a professional gets a kick out of it when he smashes a long, straight tee shot far down the center of the fairway or sends a fairway wood shot whistling straight to the flag.

Therein, however, lies the danger. Everyone has a tendency to try to "kill it" when he steps up to a show with a wood in his hands.

Right now let me emphasize that, no matter what shot you are playing, from the drive right down to the shortest pitch, swing it sweet and let the club do the work. It seems odd and yet golf, in a way, is a game of opposites: if you want to hit it far you must hit it easy. You'll be surprised at how much better your shots will be if you get that idea firmly implanted in your mind.

THE 1-1/2 WOOD

This is the club with which I drive and I don't hesitate to suggest it for all players because of the added help in getting your tee shot "up" without conscious effort.

Too many times the casual or weekend golfer will dribble the ball along the ground, primarily because, for his swing, there isn't enough loft to the face of the club, or he will slice the ball horribly because of the wider arc of the longer-shafted driver. His timing simply isn't up to getting the clubhead around and he pulls the face of the club across the ball, giving it that slice spin.

I have had my difficulties with the driver just like anybody else.

Back in 1947, as we came up to the U.S. Open at the St. Louis Country Club, I was having all kinds of trouble with my driver. No matter what I tried, I just couldn't hit the ball consistently and I knew that my chances were cooked if I used it in the tournament.

So I left my driver in the clubhouse and used a brassie, or two wood, off the tee.

Having greater confidence in the brassie and with my timing just right, I was able to play well enough to tie

Lew Worsham for the championship. He subsequently beat me in the playoff, with a 69 to a 70, when I missed a putt on the final green.

Now this is not an alibi. But it makes my point here when I say that I was giving away too much yardage off the tees.

Since then I have shifted to the one and one-half driving wood which I have suggested for general use. This is the regulation driver, as I pointed out before, but it has more loft to the face while still not being as shallow as the brassie.

All of your wood shots require fine timing because of the longer shaft and necessarily wider arc than is used when hitting iron shots.

It is a general fault, particularly among poorer players, that not enough time is taken on the backswing. The tendency is to rush the clubhead back and fire away all in the same motion. You can't do this with the woods and hit them well. To overcome this rushing habit, go out on the practice tee and make yourself conscious of a perceptible pause at the top of the backswing. This will get you into an automatically slower pattern.

Some players try to correct resultant faults by changing their grip. But you must remember that two wrongs don't make a right.

Also remember that you, of necessity, are winding up a bit more with the woods. Thus, because of the longer shaft, you must have that much more body turn to give the club time to complete its longer arc. This makes your position, and balance, at the top of the backswing just that much more important.

Snead's stance for playing the driver.

If you hum a bar of a waltz tune, that cadence will give you an idea of how the timing with the woods should go. Bear in mind, meanwhile, that balance and coordination are, along with your timing, the main principles.

It's sort of like Ted Williams hitting a baseball. When the pitcher throws a slow curve, you'll notice that Williams or any other top hitter times his swing differently than when he goes after a fast ball. Timing, as in any sport, is one of the secrets.

THE STANCE

For the one and one-half wood, with which I drive, in taking the stance I play the ball in a line with my left heel.

The right foot is opened, or withdrawn from the intended line of flight, only slightly.

You will note in the accompanying drawing, that the arms are not extended rigidly toward the ball. As I explained previously, if the arms are too rigid you are merely tying yourself into a knot and will find it impossible to swing freely. You must feel that the arms are reaching comfortably but with a certain loose freedom.

As an aside to those who wish to experiment with a hook or a fade, I'd like to point out that your foot position should accomplish the desired effect. For a hook, merely open the right foot more, or draw it back more from the desired line of flight. For a fade, open the left foot, or draw the left foot back from the line of flight. However, again let me advise you that it is much more desirable to learn how to hit the ball straight before attempting such experiments.

THE SWING

The swing with the woods is started with a simultaneous turn of the hips and the start of a slow, measured backswing with the arms. The hip shift does not move the head, which is the fixed axis of the swing, but simply shifts the weight to the right leg without lowering or dipping the left knee.

It is extremely important, as you start the arms back, that you do not pick up the club by immediately cocking the wrists or you will ruin your rhythm and timing. The arms are almost belt high before the wrists are cocked to generate extra power, preserving balance and creating a return pattern for the spot where, on the downswing, the wrists and hands begin to explode their stored up power into the hit. The left arm meanwhile has been kept firmly extended—throughout the backswing and downswing—without bending the left elbow and with the right elbow kept in close to the body.

Of particular note is that you do *not* permit the club to drop below the horizontal at the top of the backswing.

The top of the backswing with the woods, emphasizing the straight left arm and right elbow in close to the body. Note that the club does not drop below the horizontal.

The two most important positions in making your shot — perfection at the top of the backswing and at the end of a full follow through. The groove between these two points provides the perfect swing.

In really winding up to put everything I have into a drive, I sometimes do drop the club below the horizontal at the top of my backswing. But until your swing is completely grooved, I would shun such overswinging. If you do overswing, you probably will lose control of the club because, in all probability, you are opening the fingers of the left hand. This is going to cause you to loop the clubhead and automatically slice because you have thrown your club out of its groove in tightening your grip.

It is my theory that the hips lead the downswing. The hip shift moves the weight back onto the left side and starts the arms downward. It is automatic then for the arms to swing on through. But you will note in the accompanying drawing that the wrists still are cocked with the arms having returned to the belt-line hitting area. Only then, as the arms move those final few inches to the ball, do the wrists unleash their stored up power to throw the clubhead in against the ball.

Thus, at point of contact, the ball, hands, and left shoulder all are in a straight line.

"QUITTING" ON THE SHOT

Completing the follow through is very important and one of the duffer's greatest mistakes is in failing to swing on through to a full finish. Most poor players "quit" on the shot immediately after having made contact with the ball, simply failing to strike on through. You must continue in a full follow through which brings the head up naturally, for in this manner you are getting the full power out of your swing.

Most beginners—and high handicap players—either quit as they hit the ball or finish up with arms extended straight out toward the green. Actually they are checking their power before it has exploded fully.

In the twin illustrations, showing the top of the back-swing and the finish of the follow through, you have the two perfect positions. If you go from one to the other in a full controlled swing you have the anchor points of the perfect swing.

THE BRASSIE

Quite frequently the beginner is urged by some theorists to use the brassie off the tee, instead of the driver, on the theory that it is an easier club to play than the straight-

Front view of Snead's picture swing with the woods.

faced driver. The supposed benefits here are that the duffer will get the ball up, hit it straighter and, as a result, will gain confidence off the tee.

But there are drawbacks, too.

As I pointed out previously, the brassie's loftier face will have you "popping up" when you use a wooden tee unless your timing is tremendous. And, if your timing is good to begin with, you don't need the brassie but can use a driver.

However, if you don't have a one and one-half wood for driving, then I would have to say you are better off with a brassie off the tee than with a driver which sends the ball dribbling along the ground. You may lose a lot of yardage in the process, but at least you won't lose all of your confidence.

The stance and swing with the brassie are the same as with the one and one-half wood or the driver. The mechanics, too, are exactly the same.

THE THREE WOOD

This should be your busiest fairway wood.

The spoon, because of its increased loft, does not require as good a lie as the brassie. Because of the greater loft to the face of the three wood, the spoon will sweep the ball off of a close lie where, in using a brassie, you would have to hit a perfect downward shot certain to contact the ball before touching the turf.

Remember, reverting momentarily to the brassie, that you need an exceptionally fine, lush lie before you risk using it.

Another benefit of using the spoon is that, because it is a lighter club than the brassie, you will find it much less tiring on those once-a-week muscles you are using.

The mechanics of hitting the three wood are the same as in using the one and one-half wood—or the driver and brassie, if you use them out of necessity. The principal difference is that because of the three wood's slightly shorter shaft the ball is positioned closer toward the middle of the feet and the stance is slightly more closed.

THE FOUR WOOD

This is the club which I recommend for the casual golfer's fairway shots unless he has such a fine lie that he is certain the three wood will get the ball up for him without any sort of feeling that he must help "lift" the ball.

The four wood is the ignored country cousin of the set but it should be one of your best clubs when you need distance. On distance shots from relatively poor fairway lies, or where the ball is so far down in the fringe rough as to be almost impossible to hit with a two iron, this is your club. It will give you slightly more distance than the two iron, and is a better club with which to hold the green because of its greater loft.

Under favorable conditions, with the ball sitting up in a good lie, the shot, because of the shorter shaft than the other wood clubs, should be played slightly forward of the center line between the feet. You should use a slightly closed stance.

If the lie is close, the ball is played more toward the center so that you are certain to contact the ball first. In making this type of shot, you hit down through the ball, as if taking a divot with an iron.

This is a good time to go back to the swing and emphasize that, with all the woods, the demand is for an easy swing with a slow, easy backswing, an action built wholly on smoothness and rhythm.

The reason is that, compared with the iron shots, the woods are played in a much greater arc and thus require a much longer stroke. The distance won't come all at once. You'll spank those long, straight wood shots down the middle of the fairway only after completely coordinating those three musts—swing, smoothness, and rhythm.

Keep in mind that if you swing properly you don't have to "lift" the ball. The club will do the work if you let it.

THE FIVE WOOD

This is a club which, substituted for your two and three irons, will pay fine dividends.

Most casual golfers find the wood clubs difficult to play because of their weight and because of the extra timing called for as you try to get the clubhead to come through.

You will discover that the five wood is easy to swing, although it is swung in the same manner as the other woods, because of its shorter shaft and nice balance. Because of its increased loft, you won't have the feeling that you have to help lift the ball. And its flat sole helps you slide through the ball with power you never were able to generate in the long irons.

The five wood is played almost back to the center line, as you compensate again for a slightly shorter shaft, and with a square stance.

THE FORWARD PRESS

One of the "gimmicks" which most of the pro golfers use to get their wood play swings under way smoothly and rhythmically is the "forward press."

This is a balancing self-starter which is designed to rock the swing into motion.

The forward press is accomplished merely by bending the right knee ever so slightly forward just before starting the backswing. This turns the hips and body infinitesimally toward the hole.

The clubhead remains stationary behind the ball as the hands, pushed forward by the body motion, move an inch or so ahead of the ball.

At this point you reverse your motion, rocking into your hip shift to get the backswing smoothly under way.

This is a good method to help take off the tension at the start of the swing.

"SITTING DOWN" TO THE BALL

Most top flight golfers when addressing the ball with a wood also employ a style known as "sitting down to the ball."

This is simply the process of breaking the knees ever so slightly so that most of the body weight is on the heels. This preserves balance and lets them unleash more power throughout the sweeping, all-out swing.

SLICING

As I have warned, it is not a good idea for the novice to attempt to hit deliberate hooks and fades. He will be much better off mastering the straight ball because if you can hit the ball straight the chances are that you seldom will be in the sad predicament where you need to hook or slice.

However, there admittedly are times when the advanced player will find that the hook and the slice are advantageous shots to have in his bag either from the tee or fairway.

The slice, a "banana ball" as compared with the deliberate left to right "fade" of the professionals, is the bane of most beginners. It can be due to having taken too wide a stance, a faulty grip, too open a stance (which means with the left foot drawn back from the line of flight), from getting the hands and body into the shot too soon or from collapsing the left arm.

To be certain that you have the proper stance, make certain that your feet are no farther apart than your shoulders.

If you are getting your hands and body into the shot too quickly, this is because you are hurrying your backswing and starting the downswing with your arms before the rest of the body is ready. When this is done, the clubhead drags across the ball with the club face open or tilted back to the right. This causes a backspin which rotates the ball off to the right of the line of flight.

Then, too, if you are using a stance which is too open, you must cut across the ball and thus are making it

physically impossible to contact the ball any other way than with a slice. And if your grip is faulty, with the "V's" pointing up at your chin instead of over your right shoulder, the odds are this is your trouble.

HOOKING

Hooking the ball is just the opposite of slicing. In other words, a hooked ball travels from right to left. Many professionals use the hook intentionally with their woods and long irons on the theory that it gives them extra roll after the ball hits the ground.

But both the hook and the slice can become a bad habit if either is permitted to become a regular pattern in your game. Let me emphasize once again, and I can't do it too much, that the straight ball is the greatest shot in golf.

Snead's "sweetest swing" with the woods from a side view.

If you are hooking the ball, it can be attributed to either your grip, your stance or a swing which is too flat because you aren't bending your right elbow on the backswing.

In most cases, the grip is at fault with the hands too far over to the right. In other words, you may have the "V's" formed by thumb and forefinger pointing toward your right elbow instead of toward your right shoulder, where they should be pointing.

If it is your stance which is at fault, you probably have closed it too much. This means pulling the right foot too far back from the intended line of flight.

Another contributive cause toward hooking is playing the ball too far back from the center line, toward the right foot, instead of closer to the middle or farther forward as the case may be.

That flat swing, in which your right elbow is in at your side where it should be but the right arm isn't bending upward, also can be at fault by making you swing from the inside out and imparting the hook spin.

DIFFICULT LIES

Don't attempt to play those difficult lies—uphill, downhill and sidehill—while you are learning to groove your

swing. Otherwise you will merely be confusing yourself. Hit it from a good level spot until you are ready for serious play.

But these are the shots, once you start to play seriously, which you will have to face on every round.

THE UPHILL LIE

The uphill lie is one in which you will find your left foot

higher than your right foot. This causes a natural tendency to throw the weight back on your right foot so you must compensate for this unbalanced weight distribution by bending your left knee slightly to attain better balance.

On the uphill lie, the ball is played slightly back from the line to the left heel. Due to the weight being mostly

Playing the uphill lie with the woods, Snead demonstrates how the left leg is bent slightly for more even weight distribution.

Even with the irons, for an uphill lie the ball is played slightly back from the line to the left heel. The stance is more narrow than with the longer-shafted wooden clubs.

on the right foot, you may have a tendency to hook. Therefore, *aim* slightly to the right of your objective and open your stance the least bit.

Don't worry about getting the ball up into the air. The natural slope of the hill will help get the ball into the air, probably even more than you desire. It is a good rule to use a club with less loft than you would ordinarily, say a five instead of a six, because of this automatically imposed elevation to the shot. The ball is naturally going to have more loft so, if the distance calls for a six iron you would be better off with a five iron. Or, if it looks to be a four iron shot, you might want to go to a five wood or even a four wood, depending on the height of the rise from which you are playing the shot.

On a downhill lie, the right leg is bent for better balance and the ball is played slightly back of the center line.

The iron shot from a downhill lie calls for a slightly more narrow stance.

THE DOWNHILL LIE

This uphill practice, naturally, would be virtually reversed when playing a downhill shot in order to compensate for the differences. Here the weight is mostly on the left leg and you have a tendency to slice.

I prefer a closed stance to counteract the slice and the right knee is bent slightly for balance. The ball should be played slightly back of the center line. You will have a tendency to slice so aim a bit to the left of your objective.

In playing the downhill lie, you should use a club with more loft. This is due to the fact that you have trouble getting the ball into the air because the natural roll of the downhill position offsets some of the loft of your club.

But again permit me to caution you: let the club do the work and don't try to "lift" the ball. The club will do the job if you give it a chance.

SIDEHILL LIES

Sidehill lies are more difficult shots than either the uphill or downhill lies. They can be from either of two positions—one where the ball is lower than the feet and the other where the ball is higher than the feet.

In the sidehill lie, where the ball is lower than the feet, Snead takes a longer grip and bends the knees to keep the weight on the heels to stay down on the ball and prevent a topped shot.

When the ball is higher than the feet, the grip is shortened. The weight is on the balls of the feet to prevent falling away from the shot.

Adjustments to allow you to take a good swing at the ball actually are easy to make. If the ball is higher than the feet, simply shorten your grip on the shaft. If it is lower than your feet, take a longer grip on the shaft.

When the ball is on a lower plane, the difficulty is that you have a tendency to reach for the ball. The best means of dealing with this problem is to bend slightly at the knees to make certain that you keep most of the weight on the heels so you don't fall into the shot. You must stay down throughout your swing or you will top the ball. Also take your stance slightly closer to the ball than usual.

When the ball is higher than the feet, balance is your main problem. So, in addition to shortening your grip on the club, take your stance slightly farther from the ball than usual and keep your weight on the balls of the feet. If you do this, you will not fall away from the shot as you swing.

On the occasions when you are confronted with these various lies, think only of the variations you must make to meet the altered conditions. These are the position of the feet, where to grip the club, and what club to use.

But never alter the rhythm or timing of your swing.

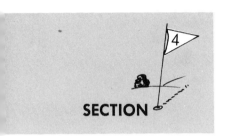

THE LONG IRONS

Now let's consider the long irons—the two and three irons—even though I recommend that the duffer shun them as if they were the plague.

Because the faces of the long irons have so little loft, most casual players have an automatic fear that the club will not lift the ball. This is a terribly difficult feeling to lose, barring a great deal of practice, which is why I suggest that if you don't have the time to work on these clubs that you leave them alone.

Snead demonstrates the square stance used when hitting the long irons, with the ball played just ahead of the center line between the feet.

The effect of this feeling is an inclination to lift up with the body in the act of hitting the ball. This produces a low-flying slice.

If you insist on playing these long irons, remember that the swing is no different than that used with the woods.

The only difference is that you stand fractionally closer to the ball. This is made necessary merely because the shafts of the two and three irons are a bit shorter than the shafts of the woods and, if you didn't move in on the ball, you would be reaching too far to meet it.

Yet in playing the two and three irons you must take a full backswing and make a complete pivot just as in wood play. It is of particular importance in playing these difficult long iron shots that you stay down over the ball and reserve the use of the hands until the club is really into the hitting area as when hitting your woods.

THE TWO IRON

This is the heavy artillery of your irons and is used for distances up to 200 yards. While I suggest that you hit the four wood in place of the two iron, let me say that the two iron will outweigh the four wood for distances up to 210 yards when you are hitting into the wind.

This is because of the fact that the four wood carries the ball higher into the air than the two iron. Therefore a four wood shot can be affected more easily by the wind. The two iron does keep the ball lower and provides less chance for the elements to interfere.

Again let me repeat, to use the two iron you must labor to master the club. For one thing, a firm grip is highly necessary. The grip, particularly at the point of impact, must be more firm with both hands than it is when hitting the woods.

The reason for this is that if you don't hold the club with extra firmness the shock of contact with the ball will cause the clubhead to turn in your hands. The heaviness of the head of the wood club helps to hold it in line against the pressure of contact with the ball. The thin blade of the

two iron—and the three iron—offers no such resistance against this shock of contact.

Another common fault with the two iron is playing the ball too far forward, or too far toward the left foot. This club should be hit just ahead of the center line between the two feet. The ball at address is played several inches back of the line to the left heel.

In taking your stance for the two and three irons, your feet should be square to the line of flight. The stance is not as wide as in hitting the woods, being narrowed as a balance factor with the ball being played closer in to the body.

This means that the long iron swing, while sweeping and full as when hitting the woods, is more compact and

Front view of Snead's long iron swing.

upright. Still you must carry out the same cardinal principles as in hitting your wood shots.

To emphasize, the clubhead is taken back low and slow, with no cocking of the wrists until the hands have left the belt line area on the backswing.

One of the basic faults in long iron play is lunging at the ball. You must eliminate the feeling that, needing distance, you have to knock the cover off the ball.

Smooth synchronization is the secret with your two and three iron shots.

The main difference between hitting the ball with the woods and your long irons is that with your irons you take a divot, the blade of the irons cutting into the turf instead

of sliding along the turf in the manner of the flat-bottomed wood.

THE THREE IRON

You probably will feel more comfortable with a three iron than with the two iron because now you are beginning to get more visual loft in the face of the club and it gives

you a feeling that the club will lift the ball without too much effort on your part.

But it still is a difficult club to master and requires a good deal of practice. Most beginners wind up with the same net result as when using the two iron: either a topped ball or a low, bouncing slice.

The reason for such disastrous results are the same as when using the two iron. The odds are that you are failing to take a full swing, are standing too far behind the ball and have such a loose grip that the clubhead is turning when you contact the ball.

Here, too, you must have an even firmer grip than when hitting the woods. And the ball should be played almost back to the center line so that the ball is struck before the divot is taken.

Remember that the swing with the long irons is just as full as with the woods and that here, also, the weight is kept on the heels with a slight knee bend to maintain perfect balance throughout the swing.

HITTING BEHIND THE BALL

You are wasting your power if you are taking your divot before striking the ball.

The reasons why you may be taking your divot first, with that resultant waste of power, may be either that you are hitting the ball on the upswing or dipping your head and falling into the ball.

If you are hitting the ball on the upswing, it is due to the fact that you are playing the ball too far forward toward your left foot.

If you are falling into the ball, you may be swaying your body and thus moving your swing out of its groove

Side view of Snead starting his downswing with the long iron

(remember that the head is the anchor of the swing); you may be bending too far over the ball instead of giving yourself room for a full, easy swing, or you may have your weight too far forward instead of back on your heels.

TOPPING THE BALL

There undoubtedly are more "topped" shots with a two iron than with any other club, meaning that the ball is

either struck on the upswing or cut into on the way down.

There are many causes which can make you top the ball: trying to lift it with "body English," flicking the wrists, looking up, failing to pivot or playing the ball too far forward.

There are two causes why the topped shot is so prevalent with the two iron. The first is, because of that fear of the straight face of the club, that you try to "pick up" the

ball with body movement. When you do this, you are failing to pivot and naturally are pulling the clubhead up out of its groove. This causes you to come down on top of the ball. There is also a tendency to play the ball too far forward, naturally making you take your divot first and thereby hitting the ball on the upswing.

Therefore the best mechanical manner to avoid topping is to take a full, easy swing and play the ball well back toward the middle line. This minimizes the possibility of "picking up" the body and also cuts down the chances of taking your divot first and bouncing the clubhead into the ball for a topped shot.

Remember, the divot should be taken after the ball is hit. The ball actually is pinched against the ground as it is struck first and is on its flight when the divot is taken.

When you see that your divot is in back of the ball, you know that you are playing the shot too much off your left foot.

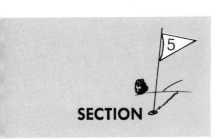

THE MEDIUM IRONS

These clubs—the four, five and six irons—are swung in exactly the same mechanical manner as the long irons.

The primary difference is that, as you work down through the set, because of the increasingly shorter shafts the ball keeps moving in closer to the feet and the swing becomes more upright.

The medium irons are double duty clubs. This is to say that they may be used with a full swing but they also are valuable—depending on your individual choice and feel—for stroke-saving chip shots.

One thing I would like to emphasize here is that in playing your medium irons, keep in mind that you should hit the ball before taking your divot. If the divot is back of where the ball was resting, you are wasting your power. The ball must be struck first and pinched against the turf before the clubhead goes on through to take the divot.

THE FOUR IRON

First of the medium irons, the four iron can be used with a full swing to cover from 160 to 170 yards. It is the beginning of the shorter range clubs which even the week-end golfer should feel confident of hitting with consistency and accuracy.

The medium iron swing is exactly the same mechanically as the long iron swing, all of the basic fundamentals being the same. Keep that left arm firmly straight and that right elbow in close to the side and never drop the club below the horizontal at the top of the backswing.

As when using the long irons, a very firm grip is necessary so that the clubhead will not turn in your hands at the point of impact.

In taking your stance for the four iron, the feet are square to the line of flight and the ball is played just a trifle ahead of the center line between the feet.

SHORT TEE SHOTS

The medium irons—the four, five and six—are the clubs which you probably will use most often for your tee shots on the shorter par three holes as well as for your approach shots from the fairway to the green.

On these types of tee shots, I would suggest that you get into the habit of eliminating the use of a wooden tee. The reason is that, in hitting this type of shot, you want to hold the green, or make certain that your ball will not bounce on the green and run on over. To make your ball hold or "bite" you will have to generate a certain amount of backspin.

This means that you must hit the ball first, then take your divot. Because only by pinching the ball against the turf with the clubhead can you impart that backspin rotation.

You will lose this backspin when you use a tee under the ball. The reason is that with a wooden tee the club slides off the ball, or vice versa, without much spin being imparted.

If you feel that setting up the ball is a mental aid, take the toe of your club and scuff up a grassy mound from which to hit your shot. Doing so, you will have both tee and backspin.

THE FIVE IRON

One of the best clubs in your bag for combined distance and accuracy, the five iron is the club for distances of anywhere from 145 to 160 yards away.

Here again the stance is square to the line of flight with the difference being that the ball is played almost squarely between the feet.

Let me emphasize once again that keeping the right elbow in against the side is vitally important. If the elbow is allowed to rise, the right arm will overpower the left arm and ruin the shot.

Keeping the left arm straight will help in this respect. At times you will observe some topnotch players permitting their left arms to bend slightly at the top of the backswing. But they have the coordination to straighten that left arm again early in the downswing so that it is firm at the point of impact.

However, rather than to fall into such a dangerous practice, I would advise that you shorten your backswing if necessary to make certain that you keep that left arm straight.

THE CHIP SHOT

The chip-and-run shot can be played with any club from the four through the nine iron, depending on the lie of the land and your personal choice.

Personally I prefer the six or seven irons, simply because I have a better "feel" with them for this type of shot.

Yet there is a great deal to the theory that you should not take a club with any more loft than you need to reach the closest edge of the green. In other words, if you are within a couple of feet of the putting surface, you can chip the ball onto the beginning of the putting surface with the four iron and run the ball up to the hole. If you are quite some distance from the putting surface, and the pin is close to the edge of the green, you might be better off with an eight or a nine iron.

The danger is in having your chip shot hit short of the green. In this case it may strike an uneven spot and bounce badly off of your selected line of flight. Therefore it is always preferable to have the chip take its first bounce on the putting surface where such bad "kicks" are not likely to occur.

Snead's narrowed stance for playing the chip shot, stance slightly open, arms straight and weight on both feet with the ball played off the right foot. The ball is struck a descending blow with a shortened grip.

In the accompanying picture, you will see the stance which I use for the chip shot. I prefer a slightly open stance, with the arms straight and the weight on both feet. The feet are rather close together, you will observe, and the ball is played off the right foot so that the ball is struck a descending blow.

No matter which club you prefer for your chip shot, the technique is exactly the same.

The face of the club is square to the line at address and the hands are slightly ahead of the ball to assure that the ball will be struck a descending blow. There should be only a minimum of wrist action when the club is taken back and on the forward part of the stroke there should be no wrist action at all. This is an arm shot, made with little body movement.

The idea, of course, is to pitch the ball as short a distance into the air as possible to reach the edge of the green and let it roll the rest of the way to the hole. You can only gauge this shot by practice and by carefully observing how the ball performs.

This is one of the shots which will save you a lot of strokes. Some over-90 shooters with whom I've played have been able to score that low only because they are pretty sharp around the greens. But the average over-90 shooter loses many saveable strokes simply because he doesn't understand how to play the chip shot.

It really is a simple shot. Just remember, you don't have to pitch the ball high up into the air. Keep it as low as you can and still have it come down on the edge of the putting surface before running up. In addition to using too lofted a club, the average player also over-pivots too much on this shot. He transfers his weight too much and then swings so fast he can't get his weight back to the ball quickly enough. As a result, he looks up, fluffs it and does everything wrong.

You should treat the chip shot as a long putt.

It doesn't matter whether you are a foot off the edge or fifteen feet or so off the carpet.

Simply play a brief, crisp little stroke, with an abbreviated backswing and equally short follow through, relying on your sense of distance to tell you how hard to hit the shot just as you would on a long approach putt.

A shorter grip, which can be noted in the drawing of the chipping stance, also should be used. By holding the club closer to the middle of the grip you will find that you have more feel and firmness and you won't be so apt to get too much distance.

No matter what club you choose, on a downhill chip shot if you open the club face slightly you will not get as much roll.

Conversely, on an uphill chip shot where you need a little more run, close the club face slightly and you will get it. In this manner facing of the club compensates for the slope of the terrain.

THE SIX IRON

Moving down to the six iron, used for distances of from 135 to 145 yards, you still use the square stance but now the ball is played slightly back of the center line between the feet.

This gradual recession of the ball toward the right foot is to make certain that—with the shaft gradually becoming shorter—you will hit the ball before taking your divot.

As with the other medium irons, keep in mind that the firm grip still is a must. This does not mean that you must clutch the club with a death grip which binds the wrists. But the grip must be firmly solid.

Another point which must be emphasized here is that you should groove yourself to use a slow backswing and make an unhurried start down to the ball—with that left arm straight. This will help you to maintain perfect balance and thereby provide complete "feel" and control of the clubhead.

CHIPPING FROM TRAPS

There are many times when it is wiser to play a chip shot out of a trap than to explode the ball. This of course depends on the lie of the ball, the lay of the land and the condition of the sand.

However, if the bank of the trap is low and there is enough putting surface between the trap and the hole—and the ball is sitting up well—it would be safer to play a variation of the chip shot in which the clubhead contacts the ball cleanly and lofts it onto the green.

This shot is played the same as any other chip shot with but two modifications. First, you hold the club as far down on the grip as is comfortably possible. Then keep your eye on the left side of the ball—enabling you to deliver a clean descending blow which, actually, is the essence of all chip shots.

SHANKING

It is in hitting the medium irons—the four, five and six—that you must guard most carefully against shanking.

Shanking is the term for a shot in which the ball is struck on the neck of the clubhead where it joins the shaft, causing the ball to scoot off at a forty-five degree angle—or worse.

There are several causes for this aggravating shot. The two major factors, however, are the choice of the wrong club and the resultant pressing.

Suppose you select a six iron for a shot on which you think that you probably should be playing a five iron. You are going to try to hit the ball for the maximum distance which you can get with the six iron.

Striving for this extra distance, the golfer tries to put extra power into his swing. Invariably this causes him to lunge toward the ball with the whole body. The clubhead is forced away from the grooved arc in which it should be traveling. The ball is hit by the neck of the clubhead—and you have a shanked shot.

A shank also can be caused by "quitting" on the shot, by a hurried backswing or by a swing with locked wrists, meaning that your wrists are stiff and failing to cock and uncock on the shot.

Any of these factors is capable of advancing the clubhead fractionally away from the body. This carries the center of the clubhead out away from the ball and drives the neck into the ball for a shanked shot.

So always take "enough club" and use a smooth, unhurried swing. You can cut down on your distance simply by shortening your grip a trifle or merely by concentrating on hitting the ball smoothly and easily.

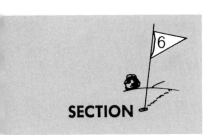

SECTION

THE SHORT IRONS

The short irons—the seven, eight and nine irons—are the real stroke savers of your set along with the wedges, which will be treated separately. These are the clubs which you should be able to hit with enough consistency and precision to put you within one-putt distance of the cup.

Bear in mind here again that in the short iron swing the basic principles are the same as with all other shots. You must take the club back without "picking it up," cocking the wrists only after you are through the belt line hitting area; the left arm is kept straight throughout the backswing, and the right elbow is in close to the side. There is one important difference.

This is that the left heel does not leave the ground.

Snead's slightly open short iron stance, with the ball played between the center line and the line to the right heel.

I point this out to drive home the point that the short iron swing is an upright, compact swing with much less body turn than is used in hitting the longer irons.

In taking the stance—as you will note in the accompanying drawing—the feet are closer together with the weight evenly distributed on both feet. The stance is square with just the slightest suggestion of having been opened slightly and the ball is played between the center line and the line to the right heel.

THE SEVEN IRON

This is the club which is used for anywhere from 125 yards to 135 yards out and, as I said before, one of the clubs with which you should be able to pin-point the flag for terrific putt-reducing dividends.

The biggest mistake that most novices make in hitting the seven iron is that they play the ball too far forward. When the shot is played in such a manner, the club reaches the bottom of the arc before it reaches the ball, wasting your power on the turf. This also is the principal reason why so many players are cursed with a fade when they play the seven iron.

BACKSPIN

It is with these short irons that you will find it important to have backspin on the ball to make it hold the green, or stop quickly. This may be necessary even on shorter shots which are governed by a shorter backswing.

Imparting this backspin is not difficult if you will keep in mind that the ball simply must be struck first with a downward blow—before taking your divot.

This means that naturally the shot must be played off a line from the right foot so that the club will necessarily contact the ball before hitting the turf.

The first few times you hit a shot with backspin you will feel as if you have struck the ball too hard. However, you soon will feel confident about hitting this shot when you see the ball "put on the brakes."

In hitting this "sit down" shot, you will undoubtedly be more effective with it when using the heavier-soled eight or nine irons. But you'll want to get that backspin action with the seven iron, too, because this is the first of those pin-pointing clubs which are going to put you close enough to the cup for a sinkable putt.

THE EIGHT IRON

With the full eight iron, you are trying for those final 110 to 125 yards with trap-dodging accuracy. Just remember that, when handled properly, it will do a consistent job.

You will notice that the hands pass close to the body as the ball is struck and that the left side shifts out of the way for an unimpeded follow through. This is, because of the shorter shafts, the ball is being played in closer.

This is a good time to look again at the full follow through, for this accents the greatest fault of the average golfer in hitting his iron shots—particularly the short irons.

Front view of the short iron swing, showing how the ball is struck before the divot is taken.

The duffer ruins his short iron game by simply quitting with the shock of impact.

You cannot hit a firm shot which will go true to the mark if you do not follow through completely. And remember, let the club do the lifting while you keep your swing smooth and grooved.

THE RECOVERY SHOT

This is the shot you must hit to get safely out of trouble with one blow when failure may wind up costing you two or three strokes.

You will discover that the eight iron is the best club for this situation. It will take the ball up and out while at the

same time it will provide fair distance with which you can position yourself nicely for your next shot.

Remember, you cannot expect to make the same distance out of long, heavy grass which you would be able to make from the ordinary lie. The most common mistake of the average player is in trying for too much distance on this shot instead of merely making certain that they are safely out of trouble, without losing any more strokes, while at the same time putting themselves in good position for their next shot.

As a result, they either knock the ball into an even worse spot or one where they are just as badly off as they were before.

It is much better, believe me, to take the penalty for the erring shot which put you in trouble and get yourself into a position where you might be able to make it up on your next shot—or at least keep yourself from having a really catastrophic hole.

Naturally, there will be times when you can use a longer club for your recovery shot. But your best bet in most trouble situations will be the eight iron.

To hit the recovery shot, play the ball off your right foot. The swing is an upright one, with the clubhead descending to the ball first. Once again, bear in mind that the clubhead will raise the ball. So don't try to lift the ball with hands or arms or with "body english."

WATER SHOTS

In the category of the recovery shot, we have the ball which is in water.

When the ball is lying partly above the surface, this shot is played just as is the sand explosion shot—explained fully in the later section on wedge play.

But let me caution you right now, if the ball is completely under water, take the penalty and play from back of the hazard.

In this connection, let me recall the trials and tribulations of Ray Ainsley of Ojai, California, in the 1938 United States Open at Cherry Hills, in Denver.

Ray hit the ball into a creek on the 16th hole and, although it was under water, decided to play the ball out. He kept playing it out—and wound up with a nineteen on the hole, the largest score ever taken on one hole in the history of the Open.

The rules of golf say that if the ball "lie or be lost" in water, you play it from in back of the hazard with a one stroke penalty. If it's sitting up with part of the ball out of the water, play it if you choose. But if it's under water, take a tip from me—and Ainsley—and accept the one stroke penalty.

Don't, under any circumstances, do what Johnny de Forest did during the third round of the Masters in 1953.

Johnny found his ball on the edge of the brook in front of the 13th green. After carefully surveying the situation, Johnny decided that he could play the ball. Thereupon he stripped off his left shoe and sock and rolled his pants above the knee.

Next, very carefully, Johnny planted the bare left foot on the bank—and stepped into the deep water with his well-shod right foot.

THE NINE IRON

Getting the maximum out of each club, so that your entire set will form a workable and dependable unit to cope with all possible yardages, should be one of your primary objects.

It is only when you have attained the maximum-yardage judgment for each club in your bag that you will be able to eliminate indecision when it comes to selecting the proper club to use.

The nine iron is the club which you will need when faced with a shot requiring extreme elevation for any distance up to 100 yards.

In playing the nine iron, the ball should be on the line to the right heel.

Here again it must be emphasized that the left heel does not leave the ground. If you find that this is happening on your short iron swing, simply cut down on the length of your backswing.

It is in using the nine iron that you must strive for a minimum of body movement. The grip is choked, or shortened, considerably which means that the knees are flexed slightly when the ball is addressed.

Be certain, as you go into your swing, that you do not dip the left knee.

Side view of Snead's swing with the short irons, emphasizing the full follow through.

Otherwise, the mechanics of hitting the shot are the same as in your other short iron shots.

Naturally, the nine iron may be used anywhere from 100 yards out clear in to the green, for it is a versatile club which also is used in chipping, or from sand traps.

Out of traps, it is employed the same as the wedge,

which is discussed in the following section. However, you will find that the heavier-soled sand wedge will handle trap chores with much greater ease and accuracy.

As explained previously, the four or five iron is preferred for chipping if a long roll is needed or if the approach to the putting surface is smooth and unobstructed.

But for a short chip which must be halted quickly, the nine iron may be used. The choice between the eight and nine irons is one of personal preference, although the nine iron naturally will give quicker elevation and slightly less roll than the eight.

In hitting the nine iron chip shot, it is a forearm stroke from a comfortably upright stance. The weight is on both feet and the ball is played off the right foot so that the ball is struck a descending blow.

PITCH SHOTS

The nine iron, as well as the eight, is of greater value in hitting pitch shots—longer shots than the chip shot and usually carrying over a hazard.

Bear in mind that there is virtually no body movement in hitting the pitch shot because it usually is made with a half or three-quarter swing.

In taking the stance for the pitch shot, with the ball played off the right foot, your feet should be closer together than in the full short iron swing. The hands are in close to the body and the left arm is kept straight. The club is taken back with the hands and arms only—and the key to the whole shot is an exceptionally smooth backswing.

While the backswing is abbreviated, the wrists must cock slightly in hitting the pitch shot.

This is a shot with the hands—but bear in mind that you must not chop at the ball. You must let the arms bring the hands into hitting position smoothly.

Remembering that smoothness is the key, don't forget that it also is highly important to follow through fully even though there is little body movement. Most shots are flubbed when hitting the pitch shot simply because the player is too anxious to see the result. Concentrate on smoothness and rhythm and you'll soon find it is one of your best shots.

THE WEDGE

Here we have the clubs—the sand wedge and the pitching wedge—which have lowered scoring so tremendously since the Jones era of golf.

These are golf's trouble shooters, whether you are in sand, rough or merely want to hit a shot which will "sit down" at the flag.

As I explained before, it is my suggestion that you carry both types of wedges. Use a sand wedge, with its wide flange on the bottom, to get out of sand traps because that's the job for which it was designed. And have the heavy-soled pitching wedge for those trouble shots out of the rough when you are within striking distance of the pin.

Snead's open-stance address when using the pitching wedge, with the ball played off the right foot.

THE PITCHING WEDGE

Nothing probably so popularized the pitching wedge as when Lew Worsham holed out from 100 yards on the final hole to win the 1953 Tam O'Shanter World Championship.

Millions of TV watchers were tuned in on the tournament when Worsham came to the 410-yard final hole needing a birdie three for a tie. He cracked a long drive and then went to the wedge. The ball arched up, landed on the green and took three gentle hops into the cup. That eagle two gave him the $25,000 first prize.

It also gives you a clear idea of what the wedge can do.

In the accompanying illustration you will see the stance used in playing the pitching wedge. The ball is played off the right foot, with a slightly open stance, so that contact will be made with the ball before the clubhead strikes the grass.

THE CUT SHOT

In playing out of deep rough, particularly when you are near the green and must make the ball stop quickly, you will find the cut shot of tremendous value. It also comes in handy when extra height is needed.

Playing the cut shot off of solid ground, the ball should be positioned just inside the right foot with a stance so open that the body is almost facing the hole. This is to make certain that the club cuts across the ball, as in hitting a slice. The face of the club is opened wide and the ball is struck before taking your divot.

You also can play this shot out of traps when a quick stop is necessary. In this case, however, the ball is played off the left foot so that a thin cushion of sand will be taken before the ball is struck. The stroke, however, is the same—upright and down across the ball.

Snead digs in with a square stance when playing the sand wedge. The ball is played off the left heel, with an open club face, to assure hitting behind the ball.

This is not a shot which is easily mastered but one which requires a great deal of practice. However, it is an extremely valuable one if you have the time to practice it.

THE SAND WEDGE

This is the shot on which you do NOT hit the ball.

Your object is to hit behind the ball, striking the sand. The force of the sand exploding against the ball pushes—or explodes—the ball into the air.

First let's consider the mechanics of the explosion shot.

The stance is taken with the ball played off the left heel and the face of the club opened. This is to assure that you will strike the sand behind the ball.

Note too, that the feet must be dug firmly into the sand for a solid footing.

The most important mechanical feature of the explosion shot is slowing the action for precise timing and swinging on through the shot.

That lazy timing is one of the top secrets of professional success with this shot. Because this is not a brute force shot but one of extreme finesse.

Take care in making the trap shot that there is little leg action. The club is taken back with the straight left arm, as in all your other shots, but observe in particular the full follow through.

Most players make their greatest mistake out of traps by quitting on the follow through once the club has driven into the sand. Don't simply bury the clubhead. Remember you are trying to drive under and through the ball.

Front view of Snead swinging on through with the sand wedge.

Nor is it necessary to try to "lift" the ball. The loft and weight of the club will take care of that job if you just swing on through.

There are three important factors in hitting the trap shot—distance required, texture of the sand and the lie.

Distance is determined not by the length of the back-swing but by the hand speed which you generate through

the ball. Only practice can tell you how much force is required for given distances.

SAND TEXTURE

Grounding the club in a trap before hitting your shot is against the rules and, of course, calls for a penalty. But you can determine the texture and condition of the sand

as you walk to your shot or as you plant your feet for a firm footing.

In the normal trap of fairly loose and dry sand, you will find it best to hit anywhere from one to two inches behind the ball.

If the sand is exceptionally soft and fluffy, a condition you will not encounter very often, you must hit closer to the ball. This is, of course, a very precise and dangerous shot.

The harder—or the wetter—the sand, the farther behind the ball you must hit. In some cases you may have to hit as much as four inches behind the ball because of the concrete-impact quality of the sand which you are exploding against the ball.

Under normal conditions, let's look at the four types of shots which you will be called upon to play most often:

AVERAGE SHOT

As explained before, this is played off the left foot with an open face. The swing is upright and "lazy," with quick wrist action at impact. Hit from one to two inches in back of the ball and follow through fully.

BURIED LIE

This is played more from the middle of the stance because you must dig down under the ball. It will help to get the ball up if you close the clubface slightly. The swing must have more action to power on through the

Side view of Snead hitting the sand wedge.

sand. Here again you hit about one to two inches behind the ball. Remember here that the ball will run more than usual so you must allow for this.

DOWNHILL LIE

In this case you have a tough shot because, ordinarily,

you are at the back edge of the trap and your carry must be long enough to get you safely out. It is complicated because your left foot is in the sand while your right foot is on higher ground. The ball must be played toward the right foot with the clubface slightly closed. Hit about two inches behind the ball with a long, full swing and a fine, full follow through.

UPHILL LIE

This time, in all probability, you are on the front edge of the trap. If the sand is not too loose and heavy, and you have a level lie with no lip on the trap between you and the green, you can use a putter advantageously.

This shot is struck much in the manner of a long putt. When using the putter, however, a flat arm motion is always best for the stroke. This brings the blade of the putter into the ball parallel with the sand. If you should use a putter and hit the ball either on the upswing or the downswing, you are likely to drive the ball into the sand.

Getting back to the wedge, for this type of shot you play the ball off the left heel with the clubface square. However, if the ball must come up abruptly to clear the lip of the trap, keep the clubface open. Here you hit two inches behind the ball and be sure to follow on through.

Most golfers are afraid of trap shots. Just remember that there is nothing to fear if you will hit behind the ball and follow on through with a full rhythmic swing.

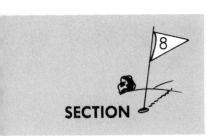

SECTION

PUTTING

Putting is a game in itself and, on the scorecard, one-half of the game of golf. Par on most courses is 72. Exactly one-half of that number of strokes for the regulation round is based on putts.

Thirty-six of those 72 strokes are expected to be taken on the putting green.

"You drive for show but you putt for dough."

That's an old saying on the pro golf circuit. It proves itself continually. Practice usually takes the kinks out of the other shots. But when you get the putting "yips" you have to overhaul your mental approach as well as your feel.

Snead's wide, square stance for better balance on long putts. The right foot serves as a prop, eyes over the ball which is played just inside the left foot.

Snead's narrowed stance for a finer touch on short putts.

For putting I use the reverse overlap grip, which merely means that the left index finger overlaps the fingers of the right hand. This is because I make the stroke with the fingers of the right hand, using the left hand merely as a guide.

There are many variations of putting grips and stances. You may find that your own individual stance suits you better than mine. If so, keep in mind that the principal idea is to be relaxed and completely comfortable when you address the ball.

However, if you feel comfortable adopting the putting stance which I am demonstrating in the accompanying drawing, I suggest you use it, as I do feel it is the best. The great majority of tournament players use this stance which, to my mind, is testimonial enough.

I do vary my putting technique by taking a wider stance for long putts. This, I feel, gives me better balance and touch when I have to strive for more distance. But on the short putts I narrow my stance considerably, as you will observe, because I feel this gives me a finer touch in pin-pointing the cup.

This is a personal idiosyncrasy and only by experimenting can you determine whether widening your stance on long putts helps in your individual case or whether you are more successful by sticking to one stance.

However, I do feel that the putting stance and form which I use is the ideal one for general use.

In taking my stance, I make sure that the weight is set up on the left side, propping myself with the right foot. The feet are even, in a square stance, and the ball is played just inside the left foot.

This is to make certain that my eyes are directly over the ball and to permit me to get my hands slightly ahead of the ball. This naturally places my hands in front of the left leg.

This is to give the ball immediate overspin as it comes off the blade of the putter. This type of action is desirable because it makes the ball hug the green as it runs toward the cup.

When your eyes are directly over the ball and your hands are ahead of it, you will necessarily get that end-over-end rotation. It is a rotation which means that the ball is contacted so squarely that it rolls "over itself," on the same vertical axis. This way there is no side spin as there would be inevitably if the ball was to be cut or pulled. A putt struck with end-over-end rotation will not spin off if it hits a corner of the cup but usually will drop home.

To tell whether you are achieving this type of rotation you can use a trick worked out by Bobby Locke, who has a tremendous putting touch. Locke daubs a line of Mercurochrome around his practice putting balls and it provides a final visual check as to exactly how the ball is rotating.

Generally there are two types of putters; the wrist-and-arm variety and the shoulder putters, who use very little wrist action. You can be effective with either style, whichever suits you best.

I find that in my case the wrist and arm style is best, although I do not use a tremendous amount of wrist action but just enough to give me a good feel of the clubhead swinging.

One of the first things on which you should work when it comes to putting is keeping the blade square, or at right angles, to the line of the putt. If you do this and stroke the ball, you can develop into a good putter and definitely improve your game.

GOING FOR THE CUP

You musn't try to hole every putt with which you are faced. As a general rule, you try only for those 20 feet or under.

On anything over 20 feet, you should strive to lag the ball up close to the cup so that you will be near enough to make the next one—and avoid those costly three-putt greens which will ruin your round. On the long putts, I don't try to hole out but merely try to get it up close to and slightly beyond the cup for a certain two-putt effort.

The man who tries to hole them all will be the man with the most three-putt greens.

Obviously, you always try to get the ball "up" to the hole but a good idea is to visualize a three foot circle around the cup on those real long ones and get the ball inside that imaginary circle.

Don't forget, however, that much of how you play that long putt depends on the contour of the green. It is generally better to leave a long putt short of the cup if the green slopes toward you. For it is much easier to make a three-footer from an uphill lie rather than from a sidehill or downhill lie.

Front view of Snead's wrist and arm style putting.

READING THE GREENS

The speed of the putt therefore is of prime importance in putting and one terrific asset in judging your speed is in learning to "read" the greens. This merely means to study the contour of the green on the path which your ball must travel and determine the bent of the grass.

As an example, if the green has been cut toward you, and the blades of grass therefore are leaning toward the ball, the putt must be stroked more firmly even against such infinitesimal pressure than it would be if the grass was leaning toward the hole.

One sign of such a condition is when the grass has a glossy sheen as you stand up to your putt. In this case the grass is bent away from you and your putt will run more freely. If the grass has a dark appearance, then in all probability it is bent toward you and the putt will require a shade more firmness.

This reading of the green is the first step which faces you when you line up your putt.

As a further example, suppose your putt must roll across a green which slopes to your left. Naturally you will have to putt up to the right to compensate for the downward roll. Yet, if the blades of grass are pointing uphill

even that slight resistance will keep the ball from rolling off as much as if the blades were pointing downhill. The ball simply will break more slowly against the grain than it will with the grain.

After determining this speed factor, you must choose the line over which you want your putt to travel.

You can determine this line much better by crouching down a few feet in back of the ball and determining the roll of the green.

One workable idea at this point is to select some shading or mark on the green a few inches in front of the ball on the exact line over which you intend the ball to travel. This will allow you to keep the line fresh in your mind and you then can concentrate on stroking the ball smoothly over that spot.

Undoubtedly one of the most common faults among average or weekend golfers is that they don't take enough time to line up their putts but merely step up and bang

Side sequence view of Snead's putting technique.

the ball in the vague general direction of the hole. It is true that a great many professionals take too long a time in studying their putts.

Jimmy Demaret said of one man who studies his putts interminably:

"He's not only studying the grain—he's reading the roots."

And yet, despite constant efforts to speed up play, let's face the fact that you may have waited all week to play

this one round of golf. So, while it isn't necessary to dally, still you should take the time to inspect the grain and contour of the green and choose your line carefully.

CONFIDENCE

The mental approach to putting is extremely important. Lacking the confidence to make a putt, you have half beaten yourself, so try to step up to your putt feeling positive and confident that you can hole it.

Negative thinking will cost you many putts which, with positive thinking, you would stroke home easily. So don't permit fear or indecision to wreck your stroke. Feel that you can do it, pick out your line, get comfortable and stroke it home.

What I'm trying to get across to you is that much of putting is mental and if you master the simple mechanics and think you can putt well—you will.

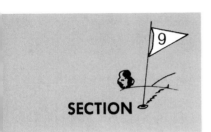

SECTION

THE PSYCHOLOGICAL SIDE

Cutting your score to an appreciable extent—particularly if you shoot in the 90's or have trouble breaking a hundred —actually is relatively easy.

Mostly it is in your head; not your aim.

Some of your trouble lies in your overt ambition; not in your swing.

The best word of advice I can give the hacker is to advise him not to attempt to hit the "pro-type" shot.

Above all, the duffer should hit the shot he knows he can hit.

Sure, the pros go for the pin. That's our job, to do some things on the golf course which you can't do. But, for the occasional golfer, the smart thing is to hit the shots you know you can hit and play your round wisely instead of gambling.

As an example, let's say you are on a 400-yard hole with no trouble near the tee. So you really unload on one with your best Sunday swing. The ball goes roughly 200 yards and now you are only 200 yards from the green. Chances are that you'll ignore the fact that there is only a narrow opening in front of the green—and that yawning sand traps are going to be grasping for your ball.

Nine times out of ten the hacker figures he'll just hit it halfway and another blast like that will put him on the green and two putts will give him that elusive par.

So what happens? Right! You wallop away and the ball rolls aggravatingly into the trap. You're three or four out of there, and maybe clean across the green and into the trap on the other side. So you two-putt for a five at best and more likely a six or a seven—or even an eight.

ME AND THE U.S. OPEN

I know what I'm talking about when I say maybe an eight. I took one once and it cost me the U.S. Open Championship. I still feel in my heart if I had won that one on that occasion, I might have won it four or five times.

It happened at Philadelphia's Spring Mill Course in

1939 and in all honesty I have to admit that I was guilty of bad thinking.

To be fair to myself, I'll have to add that I believed myself to be in a situation that day where I thought I had to gamble. Going to the tee for the 72nd and final hole, I didn't know what the leading score was. It was a long par five hole and I thought I needed a birdie four to win. That meant that I'd have to try to hit the green with my second shot.

Still, I could have played for a sure par five—and possibly have made the birdie four anyhow.

But enough "if's." As it turned out, I pushed my drive into the rough on the left and—trying to reach the green in two—yanked a two and one-half wood out of my bag. The club simply didn't have enough loft for the type of shot I had to hit and I knocked it into a fairway trap 125 yards from the green.

Taking a chance again, and trying now to get on the green in three, I tried to get out of a difficult lie with an eight iron shot. I left it. Then I knocked it into a trap just short of the green and my out—putting me on the green in five—was 65 feet from the pin. I rimmed the cup from 65 feet but then missed coming back and had to settle for that big, heart-breaking eight.

My second shot, with the two and one-half wood, was the one on which I was most guilty of bad thinking.

Had I taken a four wood, or even a two iron, I'm certain that I would have come out of it with a par five and the championship. But even a bogey six would have given me a tie.

What I'm trying to point out in recounting this story is that when you are trying to score, look the situation over well. If the odds are against a four, and you're on the border of taking a six or even worse, play for the five. Often you'll get the four anyhow by playing it safe, but at least you'll escape those double bogeys.

I played it the percentage way in 1950 and I'm sure it helped me set an all-time Vardon Trophy low scoring average of 69.23 for all of my tournament rounds.

BLUEPRINT YOUR ROUND

You can actually "blueprint" your round and save innumerable shots which you ordinarily would throw away if you gambled needlessly or tried hitting risky shots. Play those shots short of the traps, if you aren't positive you can clear them. It will leave you a little pitch instead of a desperate sand shot.

Walter Hagen, himself, played it that way on the right occasion.

"I always figured the margin of error," Hagen once said. "Anybody can blueprint a course and shoot a passable game of golf, if he doesn't knock himself out taking chances. Why, many times I deliberately played short rather than go for the green."

Playing it safe—along with an assist from Hagen's personal brand of psychology—once won the P.G.A. championship for him. It happened on the 35th hole of the finals against his old sparring partner, Leo Diegel, who at that point in the match was one up on Hagen.

It was a medium-long hole and Hagen had outdriven

Diegel by about forty yards. Diegel had a suspicion that Hagen's ball had kicked into the trees bordering the fairway but, as he started to walk ahead for a look, he saw Hagen whip out a brassie and take his stance just on the edge of the rough.

Diegel thought that Hagen had a clear shot to the green. So Leo acted like a Sunday afternoon golfer. He took a brassie, too, gave it all he had, and dumped it into a huge trap beside the green.

Hagen, after Diegel hit this disastrous shot, quietly put his own brassie back in his bag, walked into the woods from where he had an extremely hazardous shot to the green but a safe shot to an opening just short of the green —and played it safely out to the fairway just short of the trap.

Diegel came out of the trap with his third shot but needed two putts to get down.

Hagen flipped his easy chip shot to within inches of the pin and knocked it in for a four which won the hole and squared the match.

Diegel was exasperated. His irritation and resultant lack of poise helped him lose the next hole, too, along with the coveted P.G.A. championship.

PLANNING YOUR ROUND

Sometime re-examine your scorecards for a recent number of rounds and you will discover, I believe, that you have fallen into a certain pattern.

Some players score better on the front nine than on the back nine. This may not necessarily be because you are swinging better but because you lose your concentration, become distracted or tire. If your back nines are ruining your score, it is time to overhaul your mental approach.

Conversely, trouble getting started on the front nine may be due to the fact that you simply haven't warmed up. In this case, a half hour on the practice tee and the putting green before you play should iron out those armchair kinks.

And remember, careful planning of each shot as you come up to it will pay the greatest dividends of all. As Diegel discovered, it isn't being closest which counts on the scorecard. It's being safely in. Just hit your shot wisely and you'll cut down on both your exasperation and your score. Not only that, but you'll increase your luck factor, too.

Once, when Hagen hit a shot to an impossible lie, a spectator sympathized.

"Tough luck, Walter."

Hagen looked around and snorted:

"Tough luck? I put it there, didn't I?"

"BLUEPRINTING" MY BRITISH OPEN

One of my greatest thrills in golf was the day I won the British Open in 1946 at the famous old St. Andrews course in Scotland.

I didn't want to go to Great Britain for that championship in the first place. But they told me what a wonderful course St. Andrews was, and how American golf needed a good representation, and so I finally decided to give in and take a chance at it.

St. Andrews rather disappointed me at first but I changed my mind before I left Scotland. It was raw and cold, rained a good deal, was frequently misty and it blew a regular gale most of the time.

The course wasn't picturesque the way some of our American courses are, and to me it looked rather easy. But I soon found out that its easy looks belied its real character.

I found out that you had to campaign every hole AND PLACE EVERY SHOT WHERE YOU MEANT TO PLACE IT if you wanted to get a par.

This wasn't a drive and pitch course. This was a championship test.

By the time the Open started I found myself CONSTANTLY PLAYING EVERY SHOT FOR POSITION, hoping in this way to open the green for an approach which would give me a par.

The wind was terrific but it didn't bother me too much because I was successful in keeping my shots low.

In the first round, I played well, had a 71 which was two strokes under par, but still was two strokes back of Bobby Locke of South Africa, who scored a 69 on the opening round. Bobby, who had gotten away to a fine start, was one stroke ahead of Henry Cotton of England, who had an even 70.

I bettered my first round by a stroke the next day with a 70 and had a total of 141 at the halfway mark, one stroke back of Cotton, who now had taken the lead with a pair of 70's for a total of 140.

The final day the course was lengthened, the pressure was on and the wind almost blew us off our feet. I shot a 74 in the third round and, with eighteen holes to go, was tied for the lead.

The last round was rough. The galleries were large and how that wind blew! When I went out in 40 blows it looked bad but coming home I sort of got my second wind.

I SIMPLY TRIED, CONSTANTLY, TO PLAY FOR POSITION.

It paid off. On those final nine holes I dropped three birdies and went over par only once, taking a 34 for an 18-hole score of 74 and a 72-hole score of 290—four strokes better than Locke and Johnny Bulla, who tied for second place with scores of 294.

As I said before, planning your shots to avoid trouble also seems to increase your luck factor, too. It's no empty saying that you make a lot of your own luck—the good or the bad—on the golf course.

QUIT TRYING TO "KILL" IT

Everybody loves to try to knock the cover off the ball and there are times, when a hole is wide open, when you can really let loose. But if there is one particular fault which completely flattens the occasional golfer, it's the urge to knock the ball a country mile.

You'll remember Jimmy Thomson as one of the game's great hitters—yet he used a four iron off the tee a number of times in winning the $25,000 Melbourne Centenary Open in 1933.

By playing it safe, he had carved out a 10-stroke lead going to the 450-yard final hole. So, wanting to give the crowd a thrill, he took his driver—and dumped it in the woods. When he found the ball, he couldn't do anything but play straight back toward the tee.

This left him about 200 yards from the tee in two and still 250 yards from the green. An octogenarian could have been exactly even with him by hitting two feeble five irons straight down the middle.

Still wanting to show the crowd how to bust it, Jimmy took a brassie and again the ball headed for the trees. He was lucky, because it kicked out onto the fairway about 60 yards short of the green. He relaxed then—and chipped into the cup for a really scrambled four.

GUARD AGAINST LETTING DOWN

When considering the psychological side of golf, another factor of prime importance is not to let the bad shots get you down. If you feel low and disgusted after hitting a bad shot, remember Hagen's philosophy. Sir Walter always said:

"I never played without expecting to hit at least a half dozen poor shots on each round—so why should I let one bad shot bother me?"

Bear in mind that the most important shot in golf is the next one. So swing it sweet, and enjoy yourself.

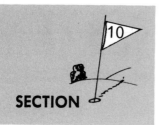

BLUEPRINTING YOUR MISTAKES

FAULT	CAUSE	CURE
BAD RECOVERY SHOTS		
	Trying for too much distance.	Use club with more loft.
	Ball positioned wrong.	Play recovery shot off right foot.
	Using "body english."	Swing freely, aiming merely for well-positioned "out."
	(See "recovery shots"— Section 6)	

FAULT	CAUSE	CURE
ERRATIC PUTTING		
(A) Off line.	Too much left hand turns blade.	Use reverse overlap, stroking with right hand. Use left as guide.
(B) Bouncing putts.	Ball "cut" or pulled.	Eye over ball, hands slightly ahead for end-over-end rotation.
(C) Three-putting.		
1. Approach putt too long.	Stance too wide; not reading green.	Narrow stance; study bent and contour.
2. Approach putt too short.	Stance too narrow; ball cut or pulled.	Widen stance for more power in stroke. Eye over ball and hands ahead for smoother ball rotation.
	(See "putting"— Section 8)	
FAULTY BALANCE		
	Improper pivot; left heel raised too high on backswing.	Shorten backswing; strive for rhythm; "sit down" to ball.
	(See "left heel"— Section 1)	
	(See "sitting down to the ball"— Section 3)	
HOOKING		
	Bad grip	Hands too "open."
	Ball played too far back toward right foot.	Play ball more forward.
	Stance too closed.	Open stance.
	Flat swing.	Get right wrist higher on backswing.

FAULT	CAUSE	CURE
	(See "grip"— Section 1) (See "hooking"— Section 3)	
LOSS OF POWER		
	Raised right elbow.	Try towel under arm.
	Quitting on shot.	Follow through fully.
	Failure to "sit down" to ball.	Weight on heels.
	Hitting behind ball.	Play ball back toward center line.
	Swaying and falling into the ball.	Pivot and swing freely.
	(See "right elbow"— Section 1)	
	(See "quitting on shot"— Section 3)	
	(See "sitting down to ball"— Section 3)	
	(See "hitting behind ball"— Section 4)	
OVERSHOOTING FROM TRAPS		
	Taking ball too cleanly.	Take more sand; from two inches or more in dry sand to four inches in wet sand.
	Ball played too far back.	Position ball off left heel.
	(See "trap shots"— Section 7)	
POOR CHIP SHOTS		
(A) Bad "kicks."	Chip hitting short of green.	Use club with more loft to take first bounce on putting surface.

FAULT	CAUSE	CURE
(B) "Fluffing."	Playing ball too far forward; looking up; downswing too rapid.	Play ball off right foot; keep eye on ball; slow backswing for easy return rhythm.
(C) Chip too long.	Too much club; grip too long. (See "the chip shot"— Section 5)	Take club with more loft or open face of club; shorten grip.
SHANKING	Trying to force power when not taking enough club.	Use club with less loft.
	Lunging at ball.	Swing freely.
	Quitting on shot.	Follow through completely.
	Stiff wrist swing. (See "shanking"— Section 5)	Cock wrists midway in backswing.
SHORT TRAP SHOTS	Taking too much sand.	Hit no more than two inches back in soft sand and no more than four inches back of ball in wet sand.
	Poor footing.	Dig feet in firmly.
	Trying to "lift" ball.	Let the club do the job.
	Ball played too far forward.	Play off left heel.
	Swing too hurried. (See "trap shots"— Section 7)	Lazy swing, with full wrist action and complete follow through.

FAULT	CAUSE	CURE
SLICING		
	Collapsing left arm.	Maintain firmly straight left arm through backswing.
	Open left hand fingers at top of backswing, causing clubhead to loop.	Feel pressure on little finger, left hand, throughout swing.
	Grip too "closed."	Check so "V's" point at right shoulder.
	Ball played too far forward.	Play more toward center line.
	Stance too wide or too open.	Close and/or narrow stance.
	(See "straight left arm"— Section 1)	
	(See "grip"— Section 2)	
	(See "slicing"— Section 3)	
TOPPED SHOTS		
	Wrong club.	Pressing or easing swing out of its groove.
	Ball played too far forward.	Move back to center line more.
	Lifting the ball with "body english."	Let the club do the work.
	Looking up and pulling swing out of groove.	Keep eye on ball.
	(See "four wood"— Section 3)	
	(See "topping ball"— Section 4)	
TENSENESS		
	Body too tight to swing.	Not enough pre-play warmup.

FAULT	CAUSE	CURE
	Arms and body tense at address.	Use waggle and forward press.
	(See "pre-play practice"— Section 1)	
	(See "waggle"— Section 1)	
	(See "forward press"— Section 3)	
WEAK PITCH SHOTS		
	Ball played too far forward.	Play ball off right foot.
	Too much body turn.	Use one-half or three-quarter swing.
	Overanxious.	Concentrate on rhythmic swing and let club do work.
	(See "pitch shots"— Section 5)	

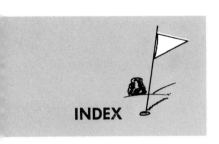

INDEX